Know Death

When You Know Death ~ You Know There Is No Death

James Mylenek Sr.

Author: James Mylenek Sr.
ISBN: 979-8-9879780-2-3
Website: knowdeath.org
Email: info@knowdeath.org

Contents

Know Death

Introduction

I remember being a young boy when I first understood what it meant to die. I wasn't afraid, just deeply curious. What puzzled me most was why everyone on earth wasn't trying to figure out what happens after we die. As I got older I learned that this kind of information was handled by religions, the medical field taught that when you die, your dead, end of conversation.

I'm now seventy-six years old. I've spent a lifetime searching for answers and sharing ideas with others seeking the truth about death. It wasn't until three years ago that I finally discovered something that deeply resonated with me, something that gave me clarity about what happens when we die.

This book is the story of that discovery. It includes both the information I encountered and the personal experiences that led me to the profound realization: consciousness does not die, only the physical body does.

I feel a strong calling to share my journey with you, not as a doctrine, but as an invitation to consider a different perspective. Imagine living without fear of death. That simple shift transformed my entire understanding of life.

If you are approaching death, supporting someone who is, or simply contemplating the mystery of death, I hope this book brings you peace, comfort, and perhaps a glimpse of a possibility that you might want to consider for yourself.

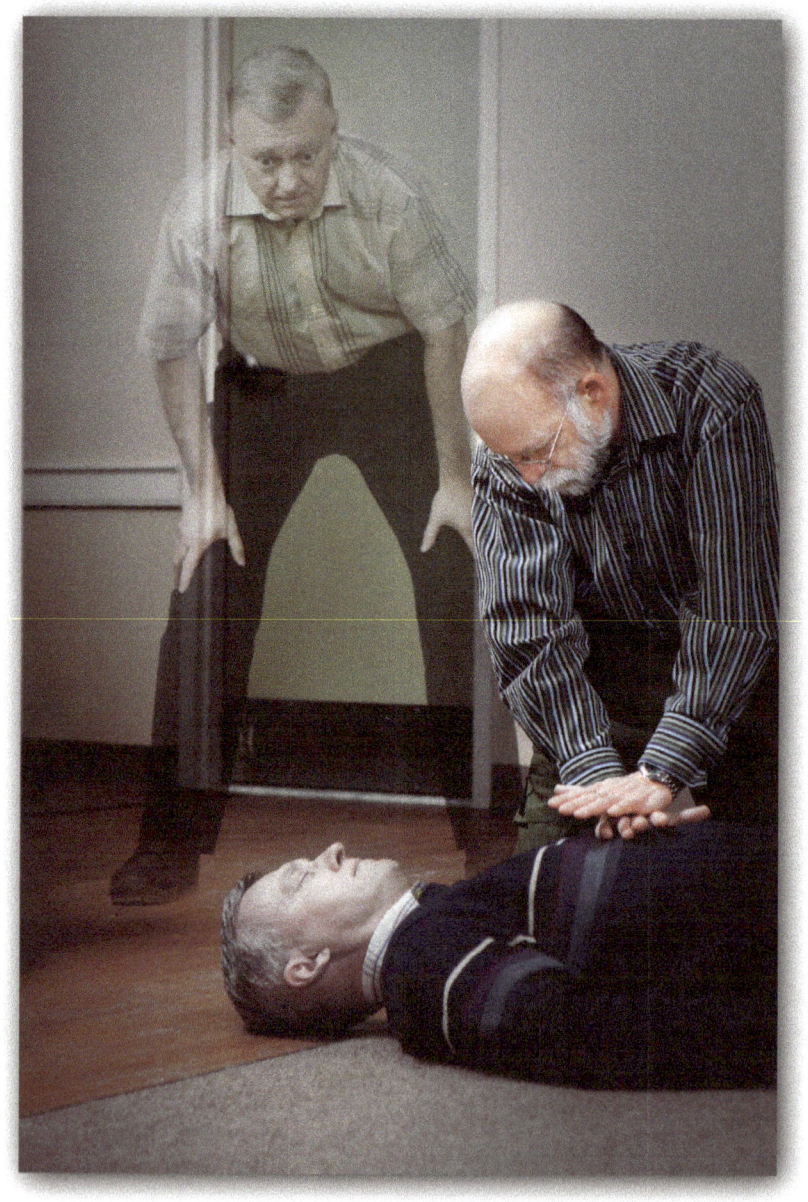

1 Near Death Experiences

Encyclopedia Britannica's definition: *near-death experience*, "Mystical or transcendent experience reported by people who have been on the threshold of death. The near-death experience varies with each individual, but characteristics frequently include hearing oneself declared dead, feelings of peacefulness, the sense of leaving one's body, the sense of moving through a dark tunnel toward a bright light, a life review, the crossing of a border, and meetings with other spiritual beings, often deceased friends and relatives. Near-death experiences are reported by about one-third of those who come close to death. Cultural and physiological explanations have been offered, but the causes remain uncertain. Typical aftereffects include greater spirituality and decreased fear of death."

I first started hearing about Near Death Experiences (NDEs) in the nineteen-eighties. At that time, the medical community was quick to dismiss them as nothing more than hallucinations, chemical reactions in the brain meant to ease the trauma of dying. The NDE stories themselves often sounded so far-fetched that it was easy to accept the scientific explanation without question.

Over time, more and more people from around the world began sharing their own NDE stories. Then, on September of 2022, I came across a podcast featuring a young man named **Vincent Tolman**. He described a powerful experience during a near-death episode, not claiming any special abilities, just a story he felt compelled to share. His sincerity struck me, so I ordered his book, "The Light After Death."

At 25 years old, Vincent and his friend accidentally took an excessive dose of a vitamin enhancer. On their way to the gym, both began experiencing severe stomach discomfort and decided to stop at a restaurant, hoping that eating something would settle their stomachs.

While at the restaurant, Vincent's friend lost consciousness. The restaurant staff immediately called 911, and paramedics were able to save him. Unbeknownst to anyone, Vincent had gone to the restroom and collapsed. He remained there unnoticed. By the time he was discovered and the paramedics arrived, he had been dead for over thirty minutes.

Declared deceased, Vincent was placed in a body bag and prepared for transport. But a young, inexperienced paramedic was overcome with a strong inner prompting, a feeling he couldn't ignore. Despite the risk to his career and in direct violation of protocol, he attempted to revive Vincent. Amazingly, his efforts worked. Vincent's heart began beating again.

Vincent spent the next three days in a coma. When he awoke, he brought back vivid memories of an extraordinary experience he had while he was clinically dead. His book tells the powerful story of what he saw and learned on the "other side."

I found the book deeply powerful, not just because of what Vincent experienced, but because of the remarkable clarity with which he remembered it and his courage in sharing it so openly. I gained a lot from reading about his journey, but what stood out most to me was how profoundly it changed his relationship with death.

Having spent so much time consciously outside of his physical body, Vincent no longer feared dying. He came back with a certainty that he was more than just his body, that his consciousness existed beyond it. To him, there was no doubt: our awareness continues after death.

After reading Vincent's book, I became convinced there was

more to NDEs than I thought and I wanted to know if his account was unique or if others had lived through a similar experience. That search led me to **Dr. Jeffrey Long**, a radiation oncologist who treats cancer with radiation and has also dedicated himself to researching NDEs.

In 1998, Jeffrey founded the Near Death Experience Research Foundation (NDERF) with a simple but powerful approach, asking experiencers directly about what they experienced. To share these accounts, he created a website, nderf.org, which has since grown into the world's largest collection of NDE stories. Today, the site hosts over 5,300 firsthand testimonials in more than thirty languages. Anyone can visit, read these accounts for themselves, and reflect on how such experiences may shape their own perspective on NDEs.

As a result of his research, Jeffrey is the author of the New York Times best seller, "Evidence of the Afterlife: The Science of Near-Death Experiences." He also wrote "God and the Afterlife: The Groundbreaking New Evidence for God and Near-Death Experience." After over twenty-five years and more than five thousand NDE first hand reports, Jeff is very well versed on the subject. I 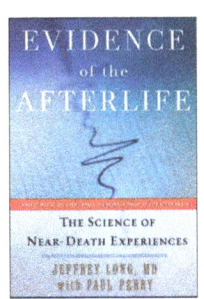 recently saw an interview with Jeffrey that was very profound and it ended with him saying,

"You know I'm a doctor, and as a cancer doctor, I know we all can rightly be concerned about the dying process. We can be concerned about the death of the people we love, and that's a loss. And, obviously, there is gonna be grief. But as far as having a fear of death in the sense of, is death going to be the end? Is there not gonna be an afterlife? Oh, heck no.

I know darn good and well, based on and we haven't even literally touched the surface of the mountain of evidence of near death experiences and other experiences that I've studied over twenty-five years. No question. Absolutely unequivocally, each and every person hearing this, we have an afterlife, a wonderful afterlife, and that's for all of us. May I add that critical understanding that there is that afterlife or we're going to be eternal souls far more than we are here, this is literally the most profoundly positive message I can conceive of to give to all of humanity."

These are just two examples among countless others now readily available to anyone exploring NDEs. A quick search online or on social media reveals an abundance of similar testimonies. What amazes me is that I had never noticed this wealth of information before, yet now, with a shift in my own awareness, it suddenly feels like it's everywhere.

Although NDEs have always existed, only in recent years have people begun sharing them more openly. For a long time, such stories were kept private, often hidden out of fear of ridicule or social rejection. Today, however, the cultural climate has changed. Curiosity is beginning to replace judgment, and what was once dismissed is now entering the conversation with growing acceptance.

Looking at where society stands now, I was surprised to discover just how many people are engaged in this subject and equally surprised that I had lived so unaware of NDEs until I began my own research.

As of now (2025), the general public's view on NDEs is a mix of curiosity, growing openness, and healthy skepticism. Here's a breakdown of how NDEs are generally perceived:

1. Increasing Acceptance

- Mainstream awareness has grown significantly, thanks to books, documentaries, podcasts, and interviews with people who've had NDEs.

- Many people now view NDEs as valid personal experiences, even if they're not fully understood scientifically.

- Polls and surveys (e.g., Pew Research, Gallup) over the past two decades suggest a steady increase in belief in an afterlife, and NDE accounts often resonate with people who hold those beliefs.

2. Spiritual and Religious Audiences

- Those with spiritual or religious worldviews are generally more open to NDEs as evidence of life after death, the soul, or divine realms. NDEs are sometimes interpreted through a faith-based lens, as confirmation of heaven, karma, or soul purpose.

3. Scientific and Skeptical Viewpoints

- Many in the medical and scientific community remain skeptical, attributing NDEs to: Oxygen deprivation in the brain or surges of neurotransmitters (like DMT).

- Psychological coping mechanisms under extreme trauma.

- The University of Virginia's "Division of Perceptual Studies" and studies like the "The AWARE Project" are examples of credible scientific inquiry into NDEs.
The Aware Project is a community education organization based in southern California that aims to balance the public conversation about psychedelics.

- That said, some researchers and doctors have become more open-minded, especially those working in cardiology, palliative care, and neuroscience.

4. Popular Culture and Media

- NDEs are a common theme in movies, books, and streaming platforms (e.g., Surviving Death on Netflix), which has helped normalize them.

- They're increasingly discussed in mental health and grief support communities, often seen as transformational experiences rather than hallucinations.

5. General Public Sentiment

- Most people don't claim to fully understand NDEs, but

many are curious and open to hearing about them. The stigma around talking about death is slowly fading, allowing more people to share their own experiences without fear of being dismissed.

Here are the statistics about the general public's views on NDEs and belief in consciousness beyond death:

Attitudes Toward Near-Death Experiences

In a Pew survey (Views on the afterlife, Nov 2021), 72% of U.S. adults said they believed it's possible for someone to have "a near-death experience in which their spirit actually leaves their body" ([seekreality.com][4]).

Similarly, over 45% report having had a "sudden feeling of connection with something from beyond this world," and 38% felt a deceased person was communicating with them ([Pew Research Center][3]).

Global Perspective

A massive Pew global survey (2024–25) spanning 36 countries found a median of 64% of adults worldwide believe in life after death; in the U.S., belief runs about 70%. ([Pew Research Center][5]).

Scientific Research & Skepticism

Studies like the AWARE project, led by Dr. Sam Parnia, found 9% of cardiac arrest survivors reported NDE experiences; only about 2% described verifiable out-of-body experiences during resuscitation ([Wikipedia][6]).

The Near-Death Experience Research Foundation (NDERF), managed by Dr. Jeffrey Long, has amassed over 5,300 firsthand NDE reports, with 95%+ of experiencers regarding them as real and trans formative ([Wikipedia][7]).

How This Shapes Public Perception Today

Most Americans are open to NDEs as legitimate phenomena,

even if they're viewed skeptically by some.

Spiritual and religious individuals often interpret NDEs as evidence of an afterlife, while many non-religious or scientific observers lean toward physiological or psychological explanations.

The increasing visibility of NDEs in books, documentaries, and mental health spaces has kindled broader curiosity and reduced stigma around talking about death and consciousness.

Summary Table

Categories	Public Response
Belief in afterlife	82%
Belief NDEs possible	72%
Connection with the deceased (dreams, presence, etc.)	40–50%
Reincarnation beliefs	27%
Medical/scientific validation of NDEs	Limited (few verified cases)

Overall, public sentiment around NDEs is characterized by curiosity and openness, alongside healthy skepticism. People increasingly regard these experiences as personally meaningful and potentially spiritually validating, even if researchers are still working to understand their underlying causes.

It now seems that the majority of people believe NDEs are real. In fact, there are currently over 130 books on Amazon dedicated to NDEs, reflecting just how widespread public interest has become.

If people are open to acknowledging NDEs, then perhaps they would also be willing to listen to those who've experienced them firsthand. And what every NDE experiencer says, without exception, is that they've lost their fear of death. It's not a belief or a hopeful idea for them. It's something they know through direct, personal experience: that consciousness continues after the body dies.

This understanding profoundly shifts how they now live. With the knowledge that death is not the end, they choose to live with more clarity, courage, and purpose, knowing that their existence will carry on beyond their physical body.

Most NDEs are powerful but relatively brief, often limited to a short glimpse outside the body and typically occurring only when someone is clinically close to death or declared dead. But now, we are going to take a significant step further into the realm of death exploration.

In the next chapter, we'll dive into Out-of-Body Experiences (OBEs), a phenomenon similar to NDEs, but with one major difference: no physical death is required.

Chapter References

[1]:https://www.hospicepalliativecaretoday.com/blogs/literature-review/2025/4/22/belief-in-an-afterlife-is-increasing-in-the-united-states-even-among-the-non-religious?utm_source=chatgpt.com "Belief in an afterlife is increasing in the United States: Even among the non-religious"

[2]:https://www.pewresearch.org/religion/2023/12/07/spiritual-beliefs/?utm_source=chatgpt.com"Americans' spiritual beliefs | Pew Research Center"

[3]:https://www.pewresearch.org/religion/2023/12/07/spirituality-among-americans/?utm_source=chatgpt.com "Spirituality Among Americans | Pew Research Center"

[4]:https://seekreality.com/seek-reality-news/most-americans-believe-afterlife-communication-is-possible/?utm_source=chatgpt.com "Americans' Belief in Afterlife Communication | Seek Reality"

[5]:https://www.pewresearch.org/religion/2025/05/06/believing-in-spirits-and-life-after-death-is-common-around-the-world/?utm_source=chatgpt.com "Spiritual and Religious Beliefs

and Practices Around the World | Pew Research Center"

[6]:https://en.wikipedia.org/wiki/Sam_Parnia?utm_source=chatgpt.com "Sam Parnia"

[7]:https://en.wikipedia.org/wiki/Near-death_experience?utm_source=chatgpt.com "Near-death experience"

2 Out Of Body Experiences

Britannica's Dictionary definition of an *out-of-body experience*: "An experience in which you have a feeling of being separated from your body and in which you can look at yourself and other people from the outside."

Out-of-Body Experiences (OBEs) are very similar to Near-Death Experiences (NDEs), with one key difference: they don't require physical death. These experiences can occur spontaneously or be initiated through specific practices or protocols. Unlike NDEs, they can happen repeatedly and last for extended periods of time.

I first encountered the concept of OBEs while watching a podcast called "Next Level Soul." This spiritual series focuses on exploring the deeper mysteries of existence, encouraging self-discovery, and helping people connect with their higher selves. The host Alex Ferrari interviewed **Darius J. Wright**, a young man who has been experiencing OBEs throughout his life.

I was genuinely amazed by what Darius had to say. If his experiences are real, the widespread ability to have OBEs could profoundly transform humanity's understanding of life and consciousness. What struck me most was his sincerity. He wasn't trying to convince anyone, just calmly sharing his direct experience.

Curious to learn more, I visited his website and explored the information he shared there. I also watched several of his YouTube videos, each one seemed more fascinating than the last. I was so inspired that I decided to sign up for his workshops.

Darius's teachings are essentially divided into two parts. First, he shares the protocol he uses to leave his body, completely drug-free. Second, he offers the insights and knowledge he's gained through years of experiencing OBEs. Darius was my first guide into this extraordinary realm. Since then, I've discovered many other teachers as well. Some use different methods, but all lead to the same profound outcome.

It's safe to say my life has been deeply transformed by this discovery. One powerful truth I feel compelled to share is this: every teacher I've encountered, and the thousands of people who've had NDEs and OBEs, all share one common realization, they've completely lost their fear of death.

Although many people today are teaching about OBEs and sharing their personal testimonials, two individuals stand out to me, particularly because of their scientific backgrounds and extensive firsthand experience. One of the most notable is Robert Allan Monroe.

Robert A. Monroe (1915-1995) was a family man, an engineering graduate, a successful American radio broadcasting executive, as well as having a distinguished career in communications, working with newspapers, magazines, and television. Unexpectedly, and without consciously seeking it, Monroe began to experience spontaneous out-of-body events. He found himself leaving his physical body and traveling in what he described as a "second body" to realms far beyond the familiar physical and spiritual dimensions of everyday life.

While continuing his successful broadcasting career, Monroe began to investigate these experiences through personal experimentation and dedicated research into expanded states of consciousness. Using himself as a primary test subject, he discovered a distinct state of awareness separate from the physical body. This phenomenon he eventually named the "out-of-body experience."

Monroe documented his early journeys in the groundbreaking book "Journeys Out of the Body" (1971), which introduced many readers to the concept for the first time. Over the next two decades, he continued to research, explore, and teach others about non-ordinary states of consciousness and practical ways to enhance human potential.

He also developed multi-day experiential workshops, enabling participants to explore these expanded realms for themselves. To support this work, he founded "The Monroe Institute," which remains active today as a leading center for consciousness research and education.

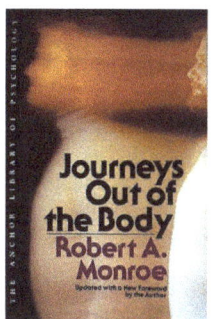

The next person that I was very impressed by is **Tom Campbell**. After obtaining degrees in mathematics and physics, Tom specialized in nuclear physics during his Ph.D. work at the University of Virginia. His 37-year professional career includes 12 years in technical intelligence, 15 years at Missile Defense Agency, and 10 years as a consultant in the general area of large-systems risk and vulnerability analysis for various high-tech companies, including two years with NASA.

In the early 1970s, in parallel to his full-time day job, Tom began researching altered states of consciousness with Robert A. Monroe. Tom, his friend Dennis Mennerich (an engineer) and a few others were instrumental in getting Robert's lab up and running. These early, drug-free consciousness pioneers simultaneously helped design experiments, developed the technology for reaching specific altered states, (binaural beats), all while being the main subjects of study.

Tom and Dennis had negotiated an arrangement with Robert, who was looking for "the right sort of scientists" to help him set up the equipment in his laboratory for the study of consciousness. Their agreement was that they would work in Robert's new lab (about 15 to 20 hours per week, in the evenings and on weekends) if Robert would teach them how to experience the larger reality. Being hardcore science-types with exceptionally high standards for evidence made Tom and Dennis challenging subjects, but Robert agreed and they began a 23-year-long relationship with Robert that lasted until Robert's passing in 1995.

Tom has been scientifically exploring and experimenting with the properties, boundaries, and abilities of consciousness ever since. These include out-of-body experiences, remote viewing, and the ability of conscious intent to modify the physical world.

Originally conceived only as a theory of consciousness, Tom soon realized that the idea of the physical universe being like a virtual reality also logically explains the supposed "weirdness" of quantum mechanics and relativity. Tom's book, "My Big TOE" derives both theories from first principles.

"My Big TOE" (**T**heory **O**f **E**verything) logically outlines the purpose of human existence, it suggests that we are components of an evolving Larger Consciousness System. Through the virtual reality game of life, we aim to enhance our individual consciousness quality, thereby advancing the system's overall evolution. While I personally haven't delved into Tom Campbell's "Big TOE" theory, his work on consciousness and OBEs is impressive, particularly given his credentials.

Tom has a website with an AI version of himself so you can ask questions at anytime. He has one-hundred and fourteen thousand subscribers on his YouTube channel with one-thousand five hundred videos. I have spent many worthwhile hours with Tom's material, this is where I learned much about death and beyond.

A growing number of researchers and OBE experiencers are sharing their insights about OBEs, their contact information is listed in the "Resources" chapter at the back of this book.

The General Public's Views on Out-of-Body Experiences

The general public's views on Out-of-Body Experiences are diverse and evolving, depending on cultural background, religious beliefs, personal experiences, and familiarity with the topic. Here's a summary of how OBEs are currently perceived by most people, especially in Western countries:

1. Growing Awareness and Curiosity

- Awareness of OBEs has increased, thanks to podcasts, YouTube channels, books, and organizations like "The Monroe Institute."

- Many people are curious but cautious, seeing OBEs as an intriguing topic even if they haven't experienced one themselves.

2. Belief Levels

- While hard data specifically on OBEs is limited, surveys on paranormal or spiritual experiences offer insight: About 15–20% of people worldwide report having had an OBE at least once in their lives (according to Gallup and other studies).

- In the U.S., roughly 1 in 10 adults say they've had an out-of-body experience.

- OBEs are generally more accepted among spiritual, New Age, and non-religious groups, and less so among traditional religious or strictly scientific communities.

3. Scientific and Medical Perspectives

- Many scientists view OBEs as neurological phenomena, often linked to:
    - Sleep paralysis or lucid dreaming
    - Temporal lobe activity
    - Trauma, extreme stress, or near-death conditions

- Some researchers have successfully induced OBE-like states in lab settings using virtual reality, magnetic stimulation, or audio protocols.

- However, mainstream science doesn't yet accept OBEs as evidence of consciousness leaving the body.

4. Spiritual and Experiential Views

- Among those who've had OBEs, the majority describe them as real, vivid, and life-changing, often comparable to near-death experiences.

- Many experiencers report:
    - A loss of fear of death
    - A shift in personal values
    - A feeling of being more than the body

- These individuals often say it's not a belief, they know from experience that consciousness does exist outside the body.

5. Public Sentiment Summary

Group	General View on OBEs
Skeptics/Scientific Minds	Hallucinations, brain phenomena
Spiritual Seekers	Valid, consciousness-expanding experiences
General Public	Curious, open but unsure; OBEs are seen as possible but unproven
Those who've had OBE	Deeply real, often trans-formative and life-affirming

Final Thought

The general public is increasingly open to the idea of OBEs, especially as more people share personal stories and as meditation, consciousness studies, and alternative spiritual practices gain popularity. While mainstream science remains cautious, cultural interest is clearly rising.

These reports clearly shows that the general public are both aware of and curious about OBEs. I was especially surprised to learn that in the U.S., approximately 1 in 10 people have had an OBE. In my own experience, whenever I bring up the topic in small groups, there's often at least one person who has had an OBE experience.

Now that I see how widespread the concept of "no death" has become, I'm surprised it hasn't received more serious research or broader discussion in mainstream media and across social platforms. Perhaps it simply takes time for these ideas to gain momentum, but it's clear to me that we're definitely moving in that direction.

In the next chapter we'll take a deeper look at what it means to live without a fear of death and explore the potential benefits and possible consequences of adopting this perspective.

Chapter References

General population incidence of OBEs (10–20%) and prevalence studies - cdc.gov, +15 - PMC +15 - ourworldindata.org +15 - Healthline +5 - aiprinc.org +5 - UVA Health Newsroom +5 - UVA Health Newsroom - IFLScience - Wikipedia

Study breakdowns about spontaneous vs. induced OBEs and mental health context - UVA Health Newsroom - IFLScience

Psychological framing of OBEs as dissociative and neurological phenomena Wikipedia +1

Death is a stripping away
of all that is not you.

The secret of life is to
"die before you die"
and find that
there is no death.

Eckhart Tolle

3 Living Without the Fear of Death

"Die before you die" refers to a spiritual concept where one lets go of their ego and attachments to the physical world, allowing for a deeper understanding of life and self before physical death. This practice encourages individuals to release their identity and fears, leading to a state of inner peace and freedom while still living.

Believing that the body dies but the soul lives on can offer several psychological, emotional, and social benefits, depending on one's cultural, spiritual, or personal framework. Here are some key benefits, grounded in common perspectives:

Comfort in Facing Mortality

This belief can reduce fear of death by providing a sense of continuity. The idea that the soul persists offers reassurance that life has a deeper, enduring meaning beyond physical existence. If consciousness is seen as continuing beyond bodily dissolution, death shifts from being an absolute end to a threshold. This can dissolve existential dread and replace it with curiosity about the next phase of the soul's journey.

Purpose and Meaning

It can foster a sense of purpose, encouraging individuals to focus on spiritual growth, moral actions, or legacy, believing their soul's journey transcends the physical world. Life's challenges and losses can be re-framed as experiences for the soul's growth rather than random suffering. This perspective often transforms hardship into purposeful initiation, reducing feelings of meaninglessness. You stop identifying too closely with your physical avatar and start seeing the bigger picture, your consciousness is on a journey of growth and learning, not just confined to one life experience.

Coping with Grief

For those grieving, the belief that a loved one's soul continues can provide solace, maintaining a sense of connection and hope for reunion or their well-being in another realm.

Moral and Ethical Guidance

Many traditions tie this belief to concepts like karma or divine judgment, motivating ethical behavior to ensure a positive outcome for the soul. When life is viewed as part of a continuum, choices take on a long arc of consequence. Ethics may then stem not from fear of punishment but from awareness that harm or harmony continues to ripple through the soul's ongoing journey.

Hope and Resilience

The idea of an eternal consciousness can inspire hope during hardships, suggesting challenges are temporary and part of a larger spiritual journey. This belief can act as an anchor in grief, making the loss of loved ones feel like a temporary separation rather than an irretrievable ending. Understanding that loved ones are still "around" in a different form can help you mourn less and celebrate their new experiences, reducing the pain of loss and allowing for a more profound connection.

Community and Cultural Connection

This belief often aligns with religious or cultural practices, fostering a sense of belonging and shared values within a community. If the soul's evolution is linked to the collective, then personal growth and helping others are not separate, they are both acts of raising the frequency of yourself and the community at the same time. Understanding that experiences, both good and bad, are opportunities for learning, you're motivated to evolve your consciousness toward love and cooperation, allowing you to make choices that enhance both your growth and that of others.

When you see others as fellow consciousnesses on their own journeys, you're more likely to act with compassion and empathy. You recognize that everyone is facing their own challenges in this game of life.

Personal Growth

Living without the fear of death can encourage self-reflection and spiritual development, as individuals strive to nurture their soul through practices like meditation, prayer, or kindness. Seeing life as a chapter in an eternal narrative often deepens appreciation for the fleeting, sensory beauty of embodiment, making each moment more vivid and sacred. Realizing you're more than your physical body means you can approach life with a sense of empowerment. It encourages you to make choices that align with your spiritual growth rather than being paralyzed by fear and societal pressures. Knowing that life is a finite experience encourages you to seize every moment, cherish your relationships, and dive into new experiences without the weight of fear holding you back. In essence, this understanding transforms life's challenges into opportunities and turns fear into freedom.

These benefits vary based on individual interpretation and cultural context. For example, in Christianity, the soul's eternal life might be tied to heaven or hell, while in Hinduism, it may involve reincarnation. Conversely, this belief might not resonate with those who find meaning in materialist or secular frameworks, where focus is on the present life only. The belief that the consciousness lives on after physical death operates less as an escape from mortality and more as a recalibration of identity, seeing oneself as more than the temporary body, while still honoring the body as the soul's current instrument.

How Does This Belief Affect My Daily Life?

Believing that only the body dies while consciousness lives on can profoundly shape daily life, influencing behavior, priorities, relationships, and overall mindset. Below, we'll explore how this belief manifests in practical ways, affecting decision-making, emotional well-being, and lifestyle choices. Many people will respond differently to this belief because of individual or cultural interpretations.

Prioritizing Meaningful Actions

Behavior: This belief often encourages individuals to focus on actions that align with a long-term view of consciousness, such as personal growth, kindness, or ethical living. For example, someone might strive to act with integrity, believing their choices impact their consciousness's future state (e.g., karma in Hinduism or Buddhism).

Daily Impact: You may dedicate time to self-improvement activities like journaling, volunteering, or learning new skills, seeing these as investments in your eternal consciousness. You might ask yourself, "How does this action reflect who I am beyond this life?" This can lead to more intentional decision-making, like choosing forgiveness over grudges or pursuing passions over fleeting pleasures. Example: A person might prioritize mentoring others, believing their influence carries forward through their consciousness of others.

Embracing Spiritual or Reflective Practices

Behavior: The belief often inspires practices aimed at nurturing or evolving consciousness, such as meditation, prayer, or mindfulness. These practices are seen as ways to connect with the eternal aspect of self or prepare consciousness for its next phase.

Daily Impact: You might carve out time each day for meditation or contemplation, fostering inner peace and clarity. For instance, someone influenced by Eastern philosophies might practice mindfulness to cultivate a "higher" state of consciousness, while a person with a New Age perspective might use affirmations to align with universal energy.

Example: A daily meditation routine could become a cornerstone of your schedule, helping you feel connected to something larger and reducing stress in daily challenges.

Shifting Perspective on Challenges

Behavior: Viewing life's difficulties as temporary or as lessons for an enduring consciousness can foster resilience. This belief re-frames setbacks as opportunities for growth rather than ultimate failures.

Daily Impact: You might approach problems with patience and optimism, asking, "What is this teaching me for my soul's journey?" This can reduce reactivity to stress, like workplace conflicts or financial struggles, and encourage proactive problem solving. You may also be less attached to material outcomes, focusing instead on emotional or spiritual growth.

Example: Someone facing a job loss might focus on learning resilience or exploring new paths, trusting that their consciousness will carry forward the wisdom gained.

Deepening Relationships

Behavior: Believing consciousness persists can lead to valuing relationships as eternal connections. People may see interactions as opportunities to create lasting positive impacts on others' consciousnesses.

Daily Impact: This might translate to more compassionate communication, active listening, or efforts to resolve conflicts. You may prioritize quality time with loved ones, believing these bonds transcend physical life. You might also seek to inspire or uplift others, viewing it as a contribution to a shared consciousness.

Example: Create a habit of expressing gratitude to friends or family daily, believing these acts strengthen eternal ties.

Reducing Material Attachment

Behavior: If consciousness is eternal, material possessions and temporary achievements may seem less significant. This belief often shifts focus toward intangible values like love, wisdom, or inner peace.

Daily Impact: Simplify your life, decluttering possessions or pursuing minimalism. You may spend less time chasing wealth or status and more on experiences that enrich your inner life, like travel, creativity, or community involvement. Make financial decisions prioritizing generosity or sustainability over accumulation. Example: Choose a lower-paying with a fulfilling career, like teaching, over a high stress corporate job, valuing the impact on your consciousness.

Facing Mortality with Peace

Behavior: The belief that consciousness endures can reduce fear of death, leading to a calmer approach to aging, illness, or end-of-life planning.

Daily Impact: You might live more fully in the present, unburdened by fear of "the end." Or engage in open conversations about death, create meaningful legacies (e.g., writing memoirs), or approach health challenges with acceptance, trusting your consciousness will continue. This can also inspire healthier lifestyles to honor the body as a temporary vessel.

Example: You might write letters to future generations or practice gratitude daily, feeling your essence will persist beyond your physical life. You might even write a book like this one.

Cultural and Individual Variations

Cultural Influence: The belief's impact varies by tradition. For example, a Buddhist focuses on daily mindfulness to break the cycle of reincarnation, while a New Age practitioner might journal to align with cosmic energy. In Christian or Islamic mysticism (e.g., Sufism), daily prayers connect to an eternal soul.

Individual Differences: Extroverts may express this belief through community service, while introverts will focus on solitary reflection. Skeptics who lean toward this belief might still live cautiously, balancing it with practical concerns.

Potential Challenges

Overemphasis on the Future: Make sure not to neglect present responsibilities, like financial planning, assuming consciousness's eternity reduces the need for worldly preparation.

Conflict with Others: This belief may clash with materialist or skeptical peers, leading to social tension or isolation if not balanced with open mindedness.

Uncertainty: Without clear evidence, some will struggle with doubt, which could disrupt the consistency of these daily practices.

Practical Example of a Day Shaped by This Belief

Imagine someone named Alex who holds this belief:

Morning: Alex starts with 15 minutes of meditation to connect with his inner consciousness, setting an intention to act with kindness.

Workday: At work, Alex prioritizes collaboration and mentorship, believing these acts ripple into their consciousness's future.

Evening: Alex journals about challenges faced, reflecting on lessons learned rather than dwelling on frustrations.

Relationships: Alex calls a friend to check in, valuing the eternal bond over temporary distractions like social media.

Night: Before bed, Alex reads a spiritual text, reinforcing his belief in consciousness's continuity and finding peace in life's impermanence.

Conclusion

The belief in life after death shapes daily life by fostering intentionality, resilience, and a focus on intangible values like growth, relationships, and inner peace. It encourages practices that align with a sense of eternal purpose, though its impact depends on how individuals interpret and balance it with practical realities.

I have found my life to be more peaceful and I'm much less likely to challenge others beliefs. I also find myself spending more time in nature, feeling in awe about this magical creation we live in. Everyone's experience will be different because everyone is different but from what I've witnessed it seems that there is benefit for everyone that seriously considers the possibility of consciousness living on after death.

How Do I Strengthen My Belief About Death?

If you have had an NDE or OBE you already know and there is no need for strengthening. But if you haven't had these experiences, strengthening the belief in the immortality of your consciousness and the distinction between physical death and conscious existence can be an enlightening journey. Here are some practical steps to help reinforce this belief:

Meditation and Introspection

Practice Regular Meditation: Set aside time for meditation to connect with your deeper self. As you can tell by now, meditation can play a big part in connecting with your higher self. I personally meditate every morning, right after I get out of bed. It helps me prepare for the day. You can also focus on the nature of consciousness and envision yourself beyond your physical body. This can help you experience and embody the belief that you are more than just a physical entity.

Reflect on Experiences: Journal about moments in your life where you felt a deeper connection beyond the physical realm, such as profound insights, dreams, or intuitive experiences.

Expand Your Knowledge

Study Consciousness: Read books, watch talks, or engage with materials that explore consciousness, spirituality, and philosophies that align with the idea of consciousness being eternal.

Explore Afterlife Experiences: Investigate various accounts of NDEs and OBEs. Read or view videos of personal testimonies that support the belief in life after physical death. I have included some of my favorites at the end of this book.

Engage with Community: Check X for recent posts on NDEs or life after death to see what others are saying.

Engage in Spiritual Practices

Participate in Group Discussions: Engaging in conversations with like-minded individuals can reinforce your beliefs and provide new insights. Forums, workshops, or online groups focused on consciousness can be great places to engage.

Visualize Your Existence Beyond Death

Create a Guided Visualization: Imagine yourself existing beyond the physical body, exploring new realms and continuing your journey. This could be a daily practice to remind yourself of your nature.

Use Affirmations: Create affirmations that resonate with your belief in consciousness, such as "I am eternal," or " My consciousness is beyond physical existence."

Face and Diminish Fear

Confront Fears: Acknowledge any fears associated with death. Write them out and reflect on how these fears aren't rooted in reality, but rather are misconceptions about your essence.

Mindfulness Practice: Use mindfulness techniques in daily living to cultivate a sense of presence and awareness, which may help reduce anxiety about mortality.

Live in Alignment with Your Belief

Embrace Fearlessness: If death is not an end, let this belief reduce fear in your daily life. Make choices that reflect trust in your eternal nature, such as pursuing meaningful goals or acting with compassion.

Practice Gratitude: Focus on the interconnectedness of all things, which can reinforce the idea that your essence is part of a larger, eternal whole. Daily gratitude for life's mysteries can help deepen this perspective.

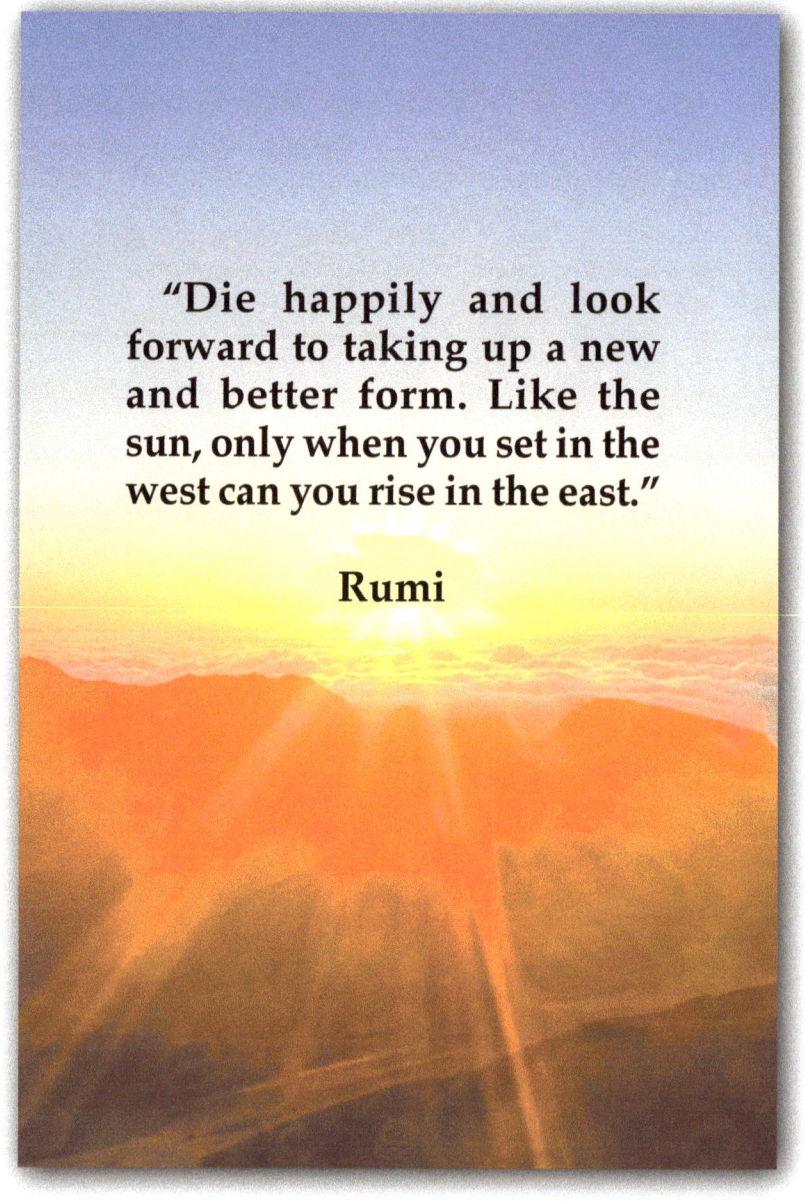

"Die happily and look forward to taking up a new and better form. Like the sun, only when you set in the west can you rise in the east."

Rumi

4 The Difference Between Believing and Knowing

There is a profound distinction between *believing* something to be true and *knowing* it from direct experience. At first glance, the two may appear similar, both shape how we see the world and how we live within it. But the gap between them is vast, and understanding this difference can change the way we approach life's biggest questions.

Belief arises when we accept something as true without having direct proof for ourselves. We may believe because it has been taught to us by family, culture, religion, or science. We may believe because an authority figure has convinced us, or because we find comfort in a particular idea. Belief has strength, but it is often tentative. It can shift when challenged by new information or shaken by doubt. Beliefs are like maps: useful for finding our way, but you don't know if it's really the right way until you get there and see for yourself.

Knowing, on the other hand, carries a certainty that comes only from experience. To know is not to speculate or to hope, it is to have walked the path yourself. When someone has an experience that transcends the ordinary, such as an Out-of-Body Experience or Near-Death Experience, what they return with is not a belief in the continuation of consciousness, but the direct knowledge of it. For them, it is no longer an idea to debate; it is a lived reality. Knowing is like standing on the mountaintop yourself, no longer relying on someone else's description of the view.

This distinction is particularly meaningful when it comes to questions of life, death, and the continuation of consciousness. Many people *believe* in an afterlife, guided by faith traditions or philosophical reasoning. But those who have stepped outside their bodies, even for a brief moment, often say the experience transformed belief into knowledge. They return not merely comforted by the possibility of survival after death, but convinced beyond doubt that they are more than their physical bodies.

The shift from belief to knowing also has practical consequences. Belief may inspire hope, but knowing dissolves fear. Those who have directly experienced themselves beyond the body consistently describe losing their fear of death. This shift changes how they live, often bringing greater clarity, compassion, and purpose. When death is no longer an end but a doorway, life itself is embraced more fully.

In this way, belief and knowing are not in competition; rather, belief can serve as the bridge to knowing. Belief motivates us to stay open, to explore, and to remain receptive to possibilities beyond our current understanding. But once an experience crosses the threshold from concept to reality, belief gives way to knowing, and knowing changes everything.

Below, I've outlined reasons why some people find belief in life after death compelling, drawing on insights from NDEs and OBEs, spiritual traditions, and philosophical ideas. I'll also address the counter perspective to help you weigh both sides.

Reasons to Consider Believing in Life After Death

1. Near-Death Experience Accounts:

Vivid Testimonies: Hundreds of thousands of people, as documented on sites like nderf.org, report NDEs involving vivid experiences of consciousness during clinical death, encounters with light, loved ones, or a sense of peace. For example, Dr. Jeffrey Long's research highlights consistent patterns across cultures, suggesting consciousness may persist beyond physical death.

Universal Themes: Common elements like out-of-body experiences, a tunnel of light, or a life review suggest a shared phenomenon that transcends cultural or religious backgrounds, lending credibility to the idea of an afterlife.

Transformative Impact: Many NDE survivors and OBE experiencers report profound life changes, such as reduced fear of death and increased compassion, which can inspire belief in a purposeful continuation of consciousness.

2. Spiritual and Religious Teachings:

Ancient Wisdom: Traditions like Hinduism (Bhagavad Gita teaches the soul's immortality), Buddhism (rebirth cycles), and Christianity (eternal life through the soul) emphasize that consciousness or the soul endures beyond the body. These time-tested beliefs provide a framework for understanding life after death.

Mystical Experiences: Practices like meditation or astral projection, often yield experiences of transcendence or connection to a universal consciousness, suggesting a non-physical existence.

3. Philosophical and Scientific Considerations:

Consciousness as Fundamental: Thinkers like David Chalmers argue consciousness may be a fundamental aspect of the universe, not just a byproduct of the brain. If consciousness is non-local, it could persist beyond physical death.

Quantum Theories: Some interpretations of quantum mechanics, like the idea of a non-material basis for reality, align with spiritual views of eternal consciousness, though these are speculative and debated.

Continuity of Energy: The law of conservation of energy suggests energy cannot be destroyed. If consciousness is tied to a form of energy, as some spiritual traditions propose, it might transform rather than cease.

4. Personal Experiences and Intuition:

Inner Knowing: Many people feel an intuitive sense of being part of something eternal, especially during meditation or moments of awe. Reflecting on these moments can strengthen belief.

Meaning and Purpose: Believing in life after death can provide comfort, reduce fear, and give life a sense of continuity and purpose, aligning actions with a larger cosmic narrative.

Counter perspective: Why Some Question Life After Death

Skeptical View: Neuroscientists like Susan Blackmore argue NDEs are brain-based phenomena, caused by oxygen deprivation or neural activity, not evidence of an afterlife. No definitive scientific proof exists for consciousness surviving death.

Lack of Empirical Evidence: Beyond personal accounts, there's no reproducible scientific data confirming an afterlife, which leads skeptics to view death as the end of consciousness.

Cultural Variation: Beliefs about the afterlife vary widely, suggesting they may reflect cultural conditioning rather than universal truth.

Why Believe? A Balanced Reflection

Personal Resonance: If NDE and OBE stories, spiritual teachings, or personal experiences resonate with you, they can form a compelling basis for belief. For example, reading NDE accounts on nderf.org, meditating, and listening to OBE teachers on YouTube might reinforce your sense of an eternal self.

Practical Benefits: Belief in life after death can reduce existential anxiety, foster hope, and inspire ethical living, as seen in NDE survivors who often embrace compassion and fearlessness.

Open-Minded Exploration: You don't need absolute proof to hold a belief. Staying open to possibilities that align with your spirituality allows you to explore without dogmatic commitment.

Ultimately, believing in life after death depends on what aligns with your experiences, values, and intuition.

My Personal Belief/Knowing

I have not personally had a NDE or a full OBE. For the past year I've been practicing techniques to initiate an OBE, but I haven't reached that point yet. However, on one occasion I did experience something remarkable, the ability to see with my eyes closed, and that alone is unforgettable.

Since first encountering this subject, I've dedicated much of my time to exploring the possibility that consciousness continues after death. This book reflects some of what I've discovered and how my belief has gradually evolved. While I've included a great deal of information here, it represents only a fraction of what I've explored over the past three years.

One thing I've noticed about those who share OBE protocols, or speak of their NDEs and OBEs, is the quality of their voice and their peaceful body language. They speak with a calm confidence… a kindness… a quiet knowing. It feels less like persuasion, and more like description. As though they are simply recounting something they are grateful to have experienced, and are glad, even excited, to share it. There is no pressure, no attempt to convince. Only an open sharing of truth, offered like a gift.

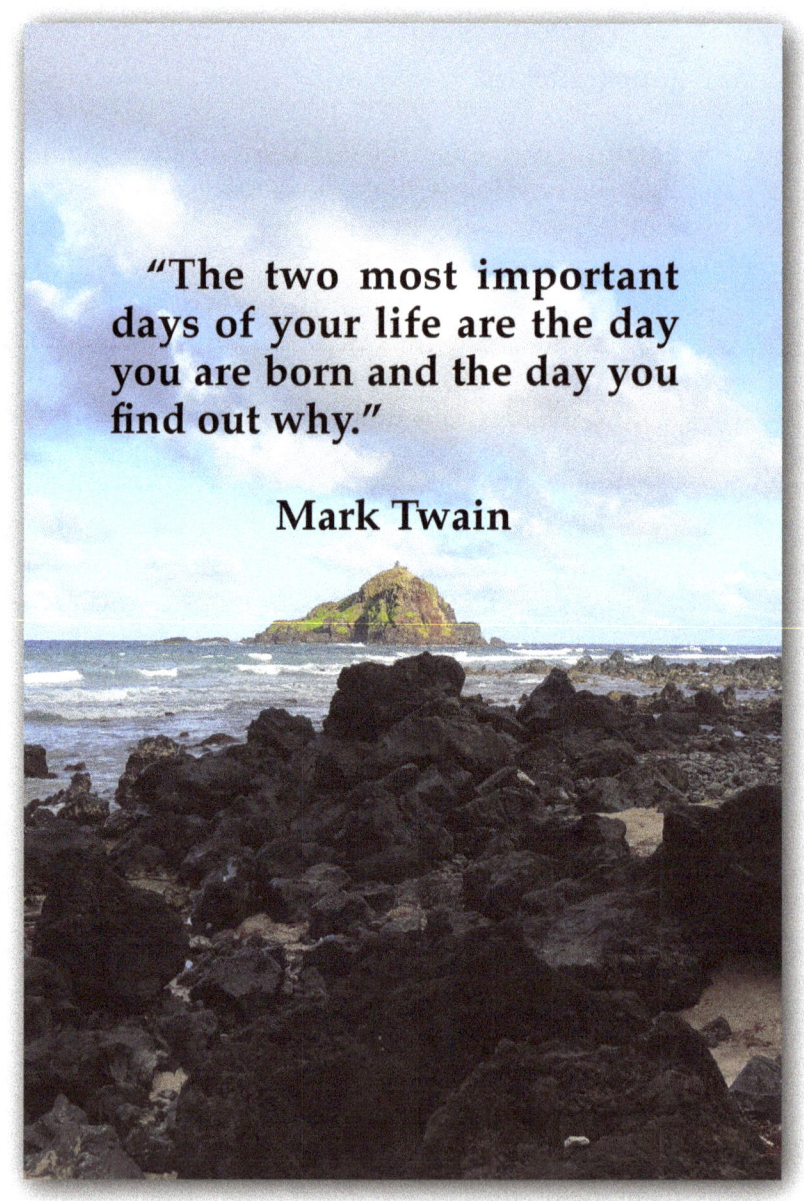

"The two most important days of your life are the day you are born and the day you find out why."

Mark Twain

5 What Does All This Mean To You?

When I look back on this journey, the stories I've read, the teachers I've listened to, and the nights I've spent trying to step outside of my own body, I find myself asking the same question you might be asking now: "what does all of this mean?"

For me, the answer is both simple and profound. I have not had a Near-Death Experience. I have not yet had a full Out-of-Body Experience. But what I have had are moments of wonder, glimpses of possibility, and the unmistakable sense that consciousness is far greater than I once imagined. Even one small moment, like seeing with my eyes closed, was enough to remind me that the boundaries of the physical body are not the boundaries of who we are.

The biggest shift for me has been in my relationship with death. For most of my life, death was the great unknown, something to fear or avoid. Now, after immersing myself in the voices of those who have crossed over and returned, and in the calm certainty of OBE teachers who explore these realms without fear, I no longer see death as an end. I see it as a transition, a continuation of a journey. And that has brought me peace.

This exploration has also reshaped the way I live. Believing that life extends beyond the body has softened my need to fight, prove, or control. I find myself spending more time in nature, more time in quiet moments, and much more time appreciating the sheer mystery of being alive.

So, what does it all mean to me? It means I no longer feel bound by fear. It means I feel freer to live with curiosity and wonder. And it means I can share this journey with you, not as someone who has all the answers, but as someone who is learning to trust the mystery.

If there is one truth I carry forward, it is this: "we are more than our bodies, and death is not the end."

A couple of days ago, after a concert, I found myself at a small gathering talking with someone I had just met. In the middle of our conversation, he shared that his wife of thirty-five years had passed away only three weeks earlier. The weight of his grief was obvious, and I felt such deep empathy for him. I wanted to offer some kind of comfort, something that might ease the heaviness he was carrying.

Gently, I asked if he held any belief about death. His answer was a simple: "No." I thought about sharing some of what I've discovered on my own journey, but I could see him beginning to close off, and he quickly changed the subject. In that moment, I knew it wasn't the time to press further. Still, I couldn't help but think that if he had even a small sense of the possibility of life after death, it might have lightened his burden, if only a little.

Approximately every half-second, someone passes away worldwide, based on an estimated 68 million annual deaths (per recent global population and mortality data). Most of these individuals likely leave behind family and friends who experience profound grief. While beliefs in an afterlife, often rooted in religious or spiritual frameworks, are held by many worldwide, the extent and nature of these beliefs vary widely. For example, major religions like Christianity, Islam, and Hinduism, which collectively represent over half the global population, incorporate concepts of an afterlife, whether it's heaven, reincarnation, or other forms. Yet, only a "small fraction" may have deep personal or experiential convictions about life after death, beyond traditional teachings.

The potential benefit of considering life after death, even for those who don't firmly believe, lies in its ability to provide meaning, hope, or a sense of continuity. Psychological studies suggest that belief in an afterlife can reduce existential anxiety and offer solace during bereavement. For instance, a 2018 study in Social "Psychological and Personality Science" found that people with afterlife beliefs often report lower levels of death anxiety compared to those without. However, skepticism or uncertainty about such concepts is also common, especially in secular or scientifically minded populations, where only about 20-30% of people in some Western countries (e.g., via Pew Research) express firm belief in an afterlife.

For the average person, even entertaining the possibility, without needing certainty, could foster resilience or a sense of connection to those they've lost. Practices like meditation, storytelling, or cultural rituals around death can help people process grief, regardless of their stance on an afterlife. Let's take a look at the current statistics.

Psychological Benefits of Considering Life After Death

The idea of an afterlife can serve as a psychological anchor for many, even if they're not fully convinced. Research, like a 2020 study in "Journal of Death and Dying," shows that people who entertain the possibility of an afterlife, whether through religious faith or personal curiosity, tend to experience less fear of their own mortality and find it easier to cope with the loss of loved ones. This is because such beliefs can:

- Provide Meaning: The notion that life continues in some form can make death feel less like an abrupt end, reducing feelings of despair.

- Foster Connection: Many report feeling a continued bond with deceased loved ones, which can ease grief. For example, practices like talking to the deceased or believing they're "watching over" can be comforting.

- Reduce Anxiety: A 2019 meta-analysis in "Palliative Care" found that afterlife beliefs correlate with lower existential distress, especially in terminal illness cases.

Even for skeptics, simply being open to the idea, without needing certainty, can encourage reflection on life's bigger questions, which can be therapeutic. For instance, journaling or discussing what an afterlife might mean can help process emotions.

Cultural Perspectives

Across cultures, afterlife beliefs shape how people grieve and find closure:

- Christianity and Islam (over 4 billion adherents combined, per 2023 Pew Research): These faiths often emphasize heaven or paradise, offering hope of reunion with loved ones. This can provide a narrative to cling to during loss.

- Hinduism and Buddhism (~1.5 billion adherents): Reincarnation offers a cyclical view of existence, where death is a transition. This can lessen the finality of loss for believers.

- Indigenous and Animist Traditions: Many cultures view the deceased as remaining spiritually present, influencing rituals like ancestor worship, which can strengthen family bonds post-loss.

- Secular Approaches: In more secular societies, like parts of Europe where only ~25% firmly believe in an afterlife (per 2022 Euro-barometer), people often find comfort in legacy, memories, values, or contributions left behind.

For the average person, exposure to these perspectives, even without adopting them, can broaden their emotional toolkit. For example, someone might not believe in reincarnation but find comfort in a Hindu-inspired ritual of honoring the deceased through storytelling.

Why It Matters for the "Average Person"

I mentioned that only a "small fraction" have strong convictions about life after death. While it's true that firm belief is less common in some regions (e.g., only ~20% in Nordic countries per recent surveys), the act of considering an afterlife doesn't require certainty. It can:
- Spark Hope: Even a fleeting thought like "What if they're still out there?" can lighten the weight of grief.

- Encourage Dialogue: Talking about afterlife possibilities

with others can build community and shared understanding, reducing isolation.

- Inspire Reflection: Contemplating what comes next can prompt people to live more intentionally, prioritizing relationships and meaning.

Real-World Impact

Given the 68 million annual deaths (roughly 186,000 daily), the ripple effect of grief is massive. If more people felt open to exploring afterlife concepts, whether through religion, philosophy, or personal curiosity, it could ease the emotional burden on millions. For instance, grief support groups often incorporate discussions of spiritual beliefs, which participants report as helpful, even if they remain agnostic.

I can only imagine how much comfort the average person might find in at least contemplating the possibility of an afterlife.

When I was younger, death typically meant a somber funeral and burial. Over time, I've noticed a shift toward "a celebration of life" that focus on honoring the person rather than mourning. More people are choosing cremation over burial, which suggests to me that they're moving away from preserving the body and visiting grave sites, embracing a less physical connection to the deceased.

What Does This All Mean To You?

It will depend on your existing beliefs about death and your openness to exploring new perspectives. That's the core of this book: offering a range of possibilities. Some ideas may resonate deeply, while others you might strongly reject, but knowing the full spectrum allows you to decide what aligns with you. Learning about NDEs and OBEs has profoundly shaped how I live my life, and I know I'm not alone.

My Lessons From Loss

Nineteen years ago, my youngest sister died. I can still recall those final two weeks we spent together, her daughters, her husband, and me, gathered around her bed. Time slowed in those days, caught between tenderness and sorrow. Eckhart Tolle's new book "A New Earth," had just come out, and I remember reading it in quiet moments, searching for something steady to hold onto in the midst of so much uncertainty. His words offered me a glimpse of a different perspective, one that suggested there was more to life, and to death, than what we'd been taught as children.

But what I remember most from those days was not only my sister's physical decline, but the weight of her fear. We had grown up in a catholic school, where nuns had instilled in us a deep fear of sin and eternal punishment. To them, almost everything seemed to be a ticket to hell. That teaching left scars, and in my sister's final days, she wrestled with the possibility that she might not be "good enough," that she might face eternal damnation the moment she took her last breath.

It was devastating to witness. I tried to comfort her, to share the sense of peace I had begun to feel from my own early explorations into consciousness and spirituality. Sometimes she leaned into my words, but other times the fear returned, pulling her back into old beliefs. Watching her suffer in that way struck something deep in me. It was unnecessary suffering, born not of truth, but of stories taught by others. That experience planted the seed that would later grow into my determination to explore questions about consciousness beyond the body.

Thirteen years later, when my mother passed away at ninety-three, the experience felt entirely different. She had been in poor health for years, her body tired and ready to let go. Though I grieved and still miss her deeply, I believed she was moving into something lighter, freer. My explorations into spirituality by that point had shaped my understanding. I didn't see her passing as an ending, but as a transition. That trust gave me a sense of peace, even as I mourned.

This past Christmas Eve, I lost another sister, my younger one, and her death revealed yet another dimension of this mystery. Unlike my youngest sister, who was consumed by fear, this sister was more open to different perspectives. About a week before she passed, I asked her whether she thought someone from our family might be waiting for her on the other side. Without hesitation, she said, "Oh yeah, I saw Mom last night. We talked and laughed for a while."

Her words stopped me. She wasn't speculating, she was reporting, calmly, joyfully, without need to convince anyone. It was as if the veil between this world and the next had already thinned for her. That moment felt like confirmation, echoing the countless NDE accounts I had studied. To her, what was happening wasn't theory. It was her experience.

Looking back, I see how each of these losses guided me deeper into my search. My youngest sister's fear revealed how destructive old religious conditioning can be, and how desperately we need a more compassionate understanding of death. My mother's passing showed me death as a release rather than an ending. And my younger sister's experience brought me face to face with the possibility that our loved ones truly meet us when we cross over.

Together, these experiences became teachers. They pushed me to explore NDEs, OBEs, and the possibility of consciousness beyond the body. They gave me reason to keep searching, reading, and practicing, not just out of curiosity, but out of love for my family, for myself, and for anyone struggling with the same fears I once saw up close.

And so, my path has become not only about studying what others report, but also about trying to experience for myself what lies beyond the physical. Because I don't just want to believe anymore. I want to know.

Why I Share This

I share these stories because I don't want anyone else to suffer the way my youngest sister did, tormented by fear in her final days. If exploring OBEs, NDEs, and the continuation of consciousness can offer even one person more peace, more openness, and less fear of death, then this journey has been worthwhile. We cannot escape the fact of death, but we can change how we meet it. For me, that makes all the difference.

If the ideas in this book about life after death have piqued your interest, I encourage you to dive deeper. The resources section at the end of this book offers a starting point to explore firsthand accounts, teachings, and perspectives from a diverse range of voices. There are teachers, young and old, from cultures worldwide, sharing insights on NDEs, OBEs, and other afterlife concepts. The key is to find those whose messages resonate with you. As you learn, you may, like me, gravitate toward new teachers whose approaches align more closely with your evolving understanding.

I hope something in these pages has spoken to you. For me, even beginning to believe, let alone to truly know, that life continues beyond the body changed everything. It shifted the way I see myself, others, and the world around me. But I soon discovered that this realization was only the beginning.

Once you accept, or even just seriously consider, that consciousness continues after death, an even bigger question arises: "What is that life like?" The next chapter explores this question in great depth, drawing on what has been discovered and shared by many who have touched that reality. I'm excited to take you there.

6 What Is Life After Death?

The ideas I'll share in this next chapter are not original claims, but reflections of concepts that have resonated with me through teachers and others I've encountered along my journey of discovery. As I mentioned earlier in this book, these are truths that feel meaningful to me, but it's up to you to explore, reflect, and decide what rings true for you. What I offer here is only one perspective among many.

Before we can explore the idea of life after death, we first need to reflect on what life itself really is. There are countless definitions, shaped by personal beliefs and experiences. What we do know is that we exist in these bodies for only a short time before moving on. Each person's journey is both unique and yet somehow similar. Many of us struggle to make sense of it all, limited by our ability to comprehend the vast mysteries of existence. After all, here we are, living on a great big ball, spinning through space in perfect harmony. We may not understand how or why, but we are here, experiencing it.

I have contemplated many ideas, but the following is the one that currently resonates with me. We are born into this world with a consciousness whose memory has been temporarily set aside. Before arriving here, we chose to incarnate in order to experience things that can only be learned on Earth. In the place we came from, there is only unconditional love and no judgment, so if we wish to understand what it feels like to be outside of love or to judge others, we must come here. That is why this world exists, so we can have these experiences.

A useful metaphor is to think of life as a play. Before the curtain rises, we choose the roles we wish to take on based on what we want to explore. We might play the hero, the villain, or anything in between. But just like actors on a stage, the roles are not who we truly are, they are only parts we temporarily embody. When the play ends, when we die, we step off the stage and return to who we really are.

So when I see someone experiencing either fame and fortune or tragedy and grief, I try not to judge them, because these are the experiences they have chosen for themselves. Part of my own journey is to offer help where I can and to celebrate with those who are enjoying the joys of life. Rather than being overly concerned with what others are doing, I focus on who I am and the experiences I came here to have.

Life, then, is our choice, to come to Earth to explore specific experiences, both physical and mental, that we ourselves have chosen. This understanding suggests that we come from our true home for the sake of these experiences, and that when we are finished, we return there. It also helps explain the length of our stay here: if we only had a few lessons or experiences to complete, our time may be short, and once we're done, we return home. With this in mind, we can now explore what "going back" or "returning home" means.

I've heard many teachers and out-of-body experiencers say that dying is like waking from a dream, relieved to find it was only a dream. For a time, that made me think life itself was nothing but suffering. But that isn't quite true either. Life reveals itself as what we shape it to be. Yes, there are certain experiences we come to earth to live through, but within them, we carry the gift of free will. That freedom allows us to choose not only how we move through those experiences, but also what we create, explore, and become in the spaces between them.

The Afterlife

What continues is the essence of who we are, the patterns of love, wisdom, choices, and growth we've built. That "you" doesn't vanish; it simply shifts form. Death doesn't end choice, it changes its context.

Many near-death and out of body experiencers describe a "life review," not as judgment, but as a panoramic remembering. In that moment, the soul can choose how to interpret, integrate, or release what was lived. It's less about "being judged" and more about choosing what to carry forward in awareness.

Path of Continuation

Some traditions describe souls choosing to return to Earth for another life (reincarnation), while others describe a choice to rest, learn, create your own world or merge more deeply into a larger field of being. In any case, the pattern of choice remains, but at a much broader scale, not tied to the limits of the body.

The Freedom of Resonance

Here on Earth, choice often feels heavy, with consequences and restrictions. After death, choice is more about resonance: you "gravitate" toward the states, people, or fields of consciousness that match your frequency. In that sense, your choices in life shape what you naturally choose after life.

So, choices in the afterlife aren't about picking from a menu of destinations. They are about how you continue to grow, integrate, or return, all guided by the resonance of who you've become through your experiences.

In the afterlife, like attracts like at the deepest level. You don't force connections, locations, or experiences, you resonate into them.

As one OBE experiencer said: "I didn't choose where to go. I simply found myself with those who felt like home, because we were the same vibration."

After death, you first arrive in realms that mirror your inner state. Loving souls enter luminous landscapes; heavy or unresolved souls may first experience dimmer, denser places until they shift resonance.

The afterlife is not about reward or punishment, it's about remembering, integrating, and continuing. It's life without the weight of a body.

Lessons From the NDE & OBE Experiencers

When people who have had OBEs describe life after death, a recurring theme appears: dying feels less like an ending and more like stepping into a larger, clearer version of life. Life after death isn't a final stop but a transition into a more natural state of awareness. It feels like returning to something deeply familiar, like home. The fear of death often dissolves because what is found is not darkness or nothingness, but continuity, clarity, and belonging.

Many describe floating above, looking down at their physical form, yet feeling more alive and free than before. The sense of "self" is not gone, it is heightened.

The body is often felt as heavy and limiting, while the out-of-body state is described as light, expansive, and effortless, like waking up from a dream. Colors, sounds, and sensations are often reported as more vivid than anything in waking life, as though physical reality was only a dim reflection of this "greater" field.

Some experiencers encounter beings of light, ancestors, or guides who communicate without words, often radiating unconditional acceptance. A number report reviewing moments of their life, sometimes with the feelings of others included, suggesting death as a continuation of learning and integration, not an end.

Once you have this experience your life changes. Knowing what happens after death has an extraordinary impact on your life here on earth. Many people who have had OBEs say that the real transformation begins after they return. The event itself may last minutes, but its impact reshapes a lifetime.

The greatest shift is often a deep release of the fear of dying. Having "been outside the body" and felt alive, people no longer see death as an end, but as a continuation. This brings a lighter, more courageous way of living.

Many return with a strong sense that relationships, love, and kindness matter more than wealth, status, or possessions. Success is redefined: not in what you own, but in how you grow and contribute.

Even if not religious before, people often become more spiritually open. They may feel guided by intuition, connected to something greater, or drawn to meditation, prayer, or study. Some report enhanced sensitivity, like being more aware of energy, emotions, or synchronicities.

People have a calmer outlook, more patience, and less interest in conflict. Greater compassion for others, because they've experienced the interconnectedness of all beings. Some lose interest in old habits (like addictions or harmful patterns) almost overnight.

Many describe returning with a mission, whether that's serving others, creating, teaching, or simply living with more authenticity. Life becomes less about surviving, and more about living consciously. The desire to share their knowledge led two people I know to become OBE teachers after learning how to leave their own bodies.

After an OBE, people often come back less afraid, more loving, more awake, and with a sense that life is precious and purposeful.

One experiencer put it this way: "Before, I was living like life was random. After my OBE, I live like every moment matters."

The following is a chart comparing many aspects of life when in the body and out of the body. The information is drawn from NDEs, OBEs, and spiritual traditions.

Life In the Body VS. Life After Death

ASPECT	LIFE IN THE BODY (EARTHLY)	LIFE AFTER DEATH (REPORTED)
Body	Biological, physical, bound by aging, illness, limits.	Subtle/energetic body—light, form shaped by consciousness.
Eating	Required for survival; food provides calories and nutrients	Not necessary; "nourishment" comes as light, love, or direct energy. Symbolic feasts sometimes reported.
Sleep	Needed for rest, repair, and dreaming.	No biological need; Consciousness remains continuous, though states of stillness or integration may occur.
Vision	Dependent on eyes, light, and distance. Can weaken or fail.	Described as 360° vision, radiant clarity, seeing in all directions at once. Colors are more vivid than earthly perception. You can "see" thoughts, emotions, and energy.
Hearing	Limited to vibration of air waves, filtered by ears.	Telepathic hearing—communication is direct, wordless, instant. Sound can be perceived as light, music, or vibration. Some report celestial "harmonies."

ASPECT	LIFE IN THE BODY (EARTHLY)	LIFE AFTER DEATH (REPORTED)
Entertainment	Often distraction or leisure, filling time. External experiences: movies, shows, games.	No boredom, no "passing time." Entertainment is shared creation, reliving memories, telling stories, or co-creating experiences for joy and insight.
Sports & Play	Physical competition; strength, skill, and rivalry. Bound by body and rules.	No bodies, no rivalry. Play becomes movement of light and thought, flying, exploring, co-creating games of pure joy, free of harm or winners/losers.
Music	Performed with instruments or voices, limited by human hearing.	Music is "infinite vibration" — light and sound woven together. Souls both create and become the music. Harmony is universal, living, and endless.
Art	Created with tools, materials, and skill; bound by physical media.	Art is instantaneous — thought becomes form. Souls paint with light, weave with energy, sculpt with imagination. Creation is fluid, ever-changing.
Identity	Tied to personality, roles, and physical self.	Expanded awareness; identity felt as essence, sometimes merging with greater wholeness.

ASPECT	LIFE IN THE BODY (EARTHLY)	LIFE AFTER DEATH (REPORTED)
Learning	Slow, through study, memory, and trial. Bound by language and time.	"Direct knowing" — understanding arrives instantly. Souls experience "life review" as teaching, and can access knowledge beyond words or books.
Creativity	Requires effort, practice, and materials. Shaped by culture, limits, and talent.	Creativity is pure expression. Thought instantly shapes reality. Souls co-create landscapes, forms, and experiences together in limitless ways.
Speaking	Requires vocal cords, breath, and language.	No need for words— thought itself is speech. Understanding is instant, no translation needed. Beings communicate essence-to-essence.
Smelling	Physical sense tied to molecules in the air.	Rarely described in NDEs, but sometimes people report fragrances of flowers, incense, or sweetness not found on Earth. Smell seems symbolic— an atmosphere of presence.
Movement	Bound by gravity, distance, and time.	Instantaneous—travel occurs through focus or intention.

ASPECT	LIFE IN THE BODY (EARTHLY)	LIFE AFTER DEATH (REPORTED)
Touching	Requires skin, nerves, and physical contact.	Touch becomes merging of energy—embraces feel like total union. There is no barrier of skin, but deep immediacy of connection. Some describe it as "touching with light."
Pain	Physical pain via nerves; emotional suffering is common.	No physical pain; emotional or spiritual discomfort possible but often met with acceptance and healing.
Time	Linear, measured by clocks and aging.	Fluid or absent—experiences feel timeless or all at once.
Sexuality	Biological drive linked to hormones and reproduction; also emotional bonding.	No reproduction or hormones; intimacy expressed as direct merging of consciousness, energy, or essence.
Romantic Love	Often mixed with attraction, need, or circumstance; shaped by roles and expectations.	Pure resonance—love without possession, jealousy, or dependency. Connection is transparent and unconditional.
Marriage	A sacred human contract, "until death," often tied to family, society, and law.	No earthly contracts; love continues beyond marriage. Souls reunite and remain connected as part of broader soul families.

ASPECT	LIFE IN THE BODY (EARTHLY)	LIFE AFTER DEATH (REPORTED)
Relationships	Can be limited by time, distance, miscommunication, or separation through death.	Instant and heart-to-heart; no distance, no secrets. Bonds deepen through direct sharing of awareness.
Union	Physical union through bodies; joy mixed with vulnerability, impermanence.	A higher union of being—described as communion, merging, or oneness, more complete than physical intimacy.
Family Bonds	Defined by bloodlines, culture, and life roles (parent, child, spouse).	Recognition and reunion of souls who have traveled together across lifetimes. Family bonds persist but are seen within larger soul networks.
Birth	Biological event: body forms, soul/consciousness enters. Marked by time, growth, and physical development.	No biological birth. Consciousness already exists in full. "New beginnings" may occur as shifts in awareness, entering new realms, or choosing reincarnation.
Death	Physical body ceases, consciousness leaves. Experienced as an ending of form.	No death of consciousness. Transitions instead: moving to higher states, joining with soul groups, or merging with Source. Some describe "death" only when choosing to reincarnate, i.e., leaving one afterlife state to enter a new embodied one.

ASPECT	LIFE IN THE BODY (EARTHLY)	LIFE AFTER DEATH (REPORTED)
Growth	Physical: childhood, adolescence, adulthood, aging.	Growth is spiritual/ energetic — expansion of awareness, integration of experiences, deepening of love and understanding
Cycle	Birth →Life → Death → (possible rebirth).	Continuity of being. Shifts in form, but essence does not end. Birth and death are seen as doorways, not finalities.
Nature	Forests, mountains, rivers, seas — limited by matter, erosion, and decay.	Living landscapes — radiant meadows, luminous mountains, rivers of light. Flowers and trees may glow or sing. Nature itself feels conscious.
Cities / Structures	Built with stone, wood, metal. Subject to time, weather, and collapse.	Temples, halls, or cities of light. Vast structures made of energy, not matter. Some describe "libraries of knowledge" or "halls of records.
Colors & Light	Colors limited to human vision spectrum. Light comes from sun, fire, electricity.	Colors beyond earthly spectrum — more vivid, radiant, "alive." Light often has presence, love, or intelligence.
Social Spaces	Families, communities, gatherings — shaped by geography and culture.	Soul groups: circles or gatherings of beings radiating recognition and belonging. Connection is instant, transparent, heart-to-heart.

ASPECT	LIFE IN THE BODY (EARTHLY)	LIFE AFTER DEATH (REPORTED)
Atmosphere	Air, sky, clouds — shaped by weather and time of day.	Atmosphere of pure resonance — no weather as we know it. Some realms are timeless day, others filled with shifting auroras of light.
Children	Born physically, grow through stages: infancy, childhood, adulthood. Vulnerable to illness, injury, death.	Appear whole, radiant, free from suffering. May be seen at a "recognizable age." Consciousness is not born so it cannot be a child. Often seen to help the transition of a loved one but loses the childhood appearance once it's not needed.
Pets & Animals	Limited by lifespan, illness, and physical needs. Provide companionship, joy, and love.	Often seen healthy, vibrant, and full of joy. Recognize and reunite with their humans. Continue as expressions of love, companions, or guides.
Clothing	Fabric garments for warmth, modesty, culture, identity, or fashion. Chosen to project an image or status.	Not physical fabric. Appears as light or thought-forms. Clothing reflects inner essence or role (robes of light, colors of resonance). Souls may appear in familiar attire for recognition, but it is symbolic, not material.

ASPECT	LIFE IN THE BODY (EARTHLY)	LIFE AFTER DEATH (REPORTED)
Truth / Lying	Lying and dishonesty are possible. People can hide feelings, deceive with words or actions.	Dishonesty is impossible. Communication is transparent — thoughts and emotions are instantly perceived. The field itself reveals truth, especially in the life review. Nothing is hidden.

Why Children and Pets Appear

When a soul first transitions, it can be disorienting. Familiar forms, a child who passed young, or a beloved pet appear as anchors of recognition. They serve as bridges, easing fear and reminding us that love continues.

In the afterlife, form is not biological, it is projected from essence and memory. Children and pets appear in the way we remember them, so we recognize and reconnect. The essence of that soul is not locked as a child or an animal, but appears in that way for communication and resonance.

On Earth, joy and culture are filtered through time, effort, and material limits. In the afterlife, they unfold as direct expressions of consciousness, limitless, playful, and shared.

In the body, our senses are bound by biology. In the afterlife, they are expanded and unified:

- You see in every direction at once.
- You hear without sound.
- You speak without words.
- You may smell or taste the essence of energy.
- You touch through direct connection of being.

On the other side, creativity and perception are no longer separate. Awareness itself becomes art, music, play, and intimacy, all woven together in the pure resonance of consciousness.

Life in the body is about survival and limits. Life after death, as described, is about continuity of awareness without those limits.

Experiencer quotes:

"It was as if all my senses blended into one. I didn't see, hear, or touch, I knew. And knowing was complete."

"The afterlife looked like Earth — but perfected. Every leaf glowed. Every color sang. It was home, but more real."

" In my OBE I felt like I had 100 big brains and when I returned to my body I had to go back to using only this little one."

What Your Afterlife Might Be

Imagine it is your last moment on Earth. Your final exhale leaves the body, and suddenly, there is a stillness. The weight you've carried all your life is gone. The body rests behind you like an empty garment. But you are awake. More awake than ever.

At first there is darkness, but not frightening, it is soft, like the night sky before dawn. Then light begins to rise around you. It is warm, embracing, not a light of the eyes, but of the heart. You feel yourself expanding into it.

You look back and see your life unfold. Every act, every word, every thought, like a river of moments pouring out at once. You feel what others felt, both the joy you gave and the pain you caused. Yet there is no condemnation, only clarity. In this seeing, you understand more deeply than you ever could in the body.

Now, notice you are not alone. In the Christian telling, this is where angels or loved ones appear, welcoming you with a love so vast it erases all fear. In the Buddhist view, luminous beings guide you through the "Bardo," showing you visions shaped by your mind and karma. In the Hawaiian way, your ancestors, your "Aumakua," stand waiting at the "Leina," the pathway of spirits, ready to walk with you. However they appear, they feel familiar. You know them. They have always known you.

The body's needs are gone. Hunger dissolves, yet you feel full, nourished by light, by love, by mana. There is no need to sleep, because awareness is continuous. You are rested in every moment, awake in a way the body never allowed.

You try to step forward, and realize, movement is not by foot, but by focus. Where you turn your attention, you arrive. If you think of a mountain, you are there. If you long for the ocean, it opens beneath you. Time is no longer measured. Moments flow in spaciousness, sometimes all at once, sometimes as gentle rhythms.

If there was pain, it has dissolved. If there was fear, it has softened into understanding. What remains is your essence, clear, free, and radiant. Some traditions call this Eternal Life, while others call it Rebirth or merging with Source. But the feeling is the same: you are part of a greater whole, and yet still yourself.

And in this greater life, you are welcomed home.

And then you realize: All the senses are not separate anymore. They weave into one seamless awareness. You don't just see or hear or touch, you know. Awareness itself is the sense.

There is no morning or evening here, but a rhythm of invitation. Something stirs within you, the pull to explore.

You are drawn into a vast open space, but it isn't built of stone or wood. It is made of resonance. The walls are woven from sound itself, shimmering like silk made of vibration. You do not hear music the way you once did. You are the music. Melodies arise around you and through you, harmonizing with other souls who have gathered. Some shine like flutes, others like drums, others like choirs, and together you create symphonies that would take lifetimes to compose on earth. Here, music never ends, because it is alive.

Next, you wander into a garden. But this is no ordinary garden, it is a gallery of living art. Trees ripple into paintings as you approach, rivers sculpt themselves into patterns of color and light.

You think of a shape, and it appears before you, blossoming like a flower. Souls around you are painting the sky, weaving tapestries of memory, sculpting visions from their imagination. Nothing is permanent, every creation shifts and flows, like sand mandalas in motion, beauty born in the moment.

You walk further and feel laughter in the air. Here souls gather not for rivalry, but for joy. They soar through the skies in playful races of light, dance in spirals across fields of energy, or join together to create dazzling patterns that radiate outward like fireworks. It feels like sports, but without scores, without loss. Just the exhilaration of movement, shared and multiplied.

Drawn forward, you arrive at vast structures rising in brilliance. They are not built of stone, but of pure energy, radiant yet soft. This is the Hall of Records, the Library of Knowing. Inside, beings of light gather in circles. They greet you not with words, but with recognition. You feel known completely. The walls themselves pulse with harmony, as if the building is alive, a temple not to worship, but to remember.

Beyond the halls, you enter a great open space. Souls gather here, glowing like constellations. Some are familiar, ancestors, friends, loved ones who passed before. Others you do not "know" in earthly terms, yet their presence feels like home. Here there is no distance, no hiding. Every thought, every feeling is shared in transparency. It is reunion beyond family, a circle of essence, a soul group.

You realize the afterlife is not one place. It is many landscapes, meadows, rivers, halls, circles, and light, each reflecting the resonance of your being.

As the experience unfolds, you realize there is no division between art, music, play, and learning. They are all expressions of the same essence, joy, love, and creation. None of it is separate from you. You are participant, creator, and witness all at once.

At last, you are lifted higher, into light so radiant it dissolves form. No landscapes now, only presence. It feels like everything you are, and everything you ever loved, has returned to the same Source. No separation, no time. Only love, endless and eternal.

And as you breathe this in, you realize: The afterlife is not an escape from earth's joys. It is their fulfillment, magnified and freed from limits.

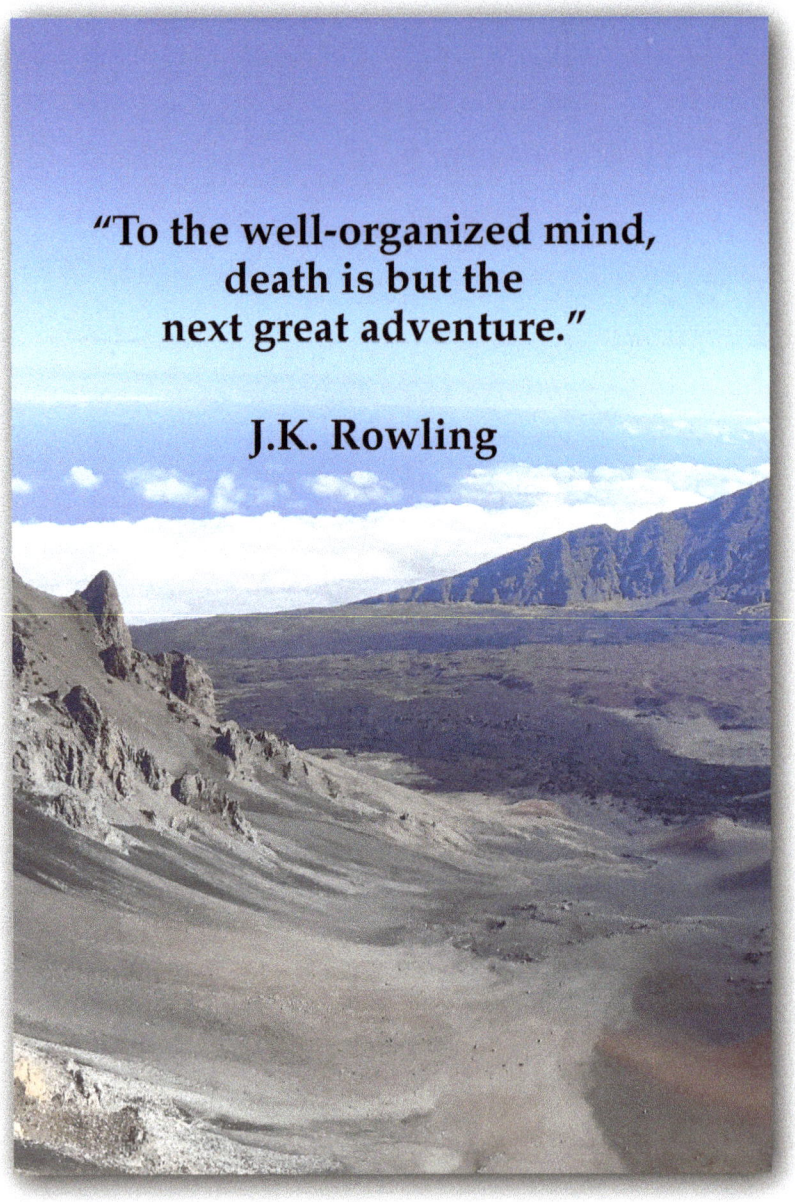

"To the well-organized mind,
death is but the
next great adventure."

J.K. Rowling

7 My Conclusion

So now you have an idea of how I came to my conclusion about life, death and the afterlife. This doesn't really feel like a conclusion though, it feels more like the beginning of a life with a new perspective of what existence really is and about how I should now live to maximize my time here on the planet in this body.

I, like many of you, have spent most of my life just trying to feed and take care of my body, live according to what society says we should be doing, and living up to the expectations of others. Fortunately we have our consciousness that can break us out of that spell and give us the curiosity and desire to know and be more.

As my life continues to unfold I continue to apply new ways of living to my remaining years. I know that before too long I will be experiencing my own OBE, and that will probably be another book or even a series. But for now, I have found a new, peaceful, and happy way to approach life's challenges, and for that, I'm forever grateful.

More and more people are becoming aware of the extraordinary experiences others are sharing and asking themselves whether these discoveries resonate within their own lives. Some begin to explore how such insights might benefit their approach to living, and what it would mean to put them into practice. The process is unique for each of us, shaped by where we are spiritually and by what we feel is necessary for our own journey while we are here.

Today, science and technology have advanced beyond anything we could have imagined, even in just the last twenty-five years. We can watch a live event on the other side of the planet or get a heart transplant by a robotic arm. Yet, for all these breakthroughs, the deepest questions still remain unanswered: Who are we? Why are we here? And where do we go when we die?

Our focus on science and technology has overshadowed the pursuit of spiritual growth. This imbalance has shaped the way we live today, and it is unlikely to correct itself on its own. If we wish to live more spiritually and seek answers to the deeper questions of life, we are going to have to do it individually alongside like-minded people in our own communities. Thankfully, the internet now makes it far easier to find and connect with one another, allowing this search to unfold much more quickly.

Even though most people continue to live as if death is the end, we can walk alongside them while choosing to live with a different awareness, knowing that human life offers the opportunity for far greater fulfillment. In doing so, we not only enrich our present lives but also expand our consciousness in preparation for the afterlife.

I know that some of you may find, in these pages, an overwhelming number of new concepts to consider and old beliefs to question. That is a good thing, because questioning and discovery are what life is about. This book is not intended to make you change your beliefs simply because I have changed mine. Instead, it offers a perspective that, for much of my life, I never even knew existed and some of you may feel the same.

As we evolve and uncover more about what it means to be human, we gain the opportunity to live more meaningful lives than the generations before us. We will still encounter the joys and challenges we came to earth to experience, but with a clearer understanding of their purpose. And that knowing can transform how we move through them. I now find myself connecting more with my eternal consciousness than my body.

It is important that we support one another as we move through our earthly experiences. Each of us can do this in our own way. For me, it has been sharing what I've learned through this book.

For you, it may be something entirely different, large or small, it all matters, and it all carries value.

By sharing this information that means so much to me, I now feel a special connection with you. I hope you have a wonderful human experience and if our paths never cross here on earth, I know, sooner or later, I'll be with you on the other side.

"This place is a dream. Only a sleeper considers it real. Then death comes like dawn, and you wake up laughing at what you thought was your grief."

Rumi

8 Recommended Resources

How to Engage

Start with the resources that feel approachable. Listen to a podcast, read a personal account, or watch a talk. Reflect on what resonates and what doesn't. As you explore, you may find yourself drawn to new perspectives that deepen your understanding of life, death, and what might lie beyond. The journey is personal, trust your instincts to guide you to the teachers and ideas that speak to you.

Out of Body Experiences: Books

Book	Title/Author	Summary
	Journeys Out of The Body Robert Monroe December 31, 1970	The definitive work on the extraordinary phenomenon of out-of-body experiences, by the founder of the internationally known Monroe Institute. Robert and the Institute have many books to choose from.
	Astral Dynamics: A New Approach to Out-Of-Body Experience Robert Bruce October 30, 1999	In this fascinating volume, Robert Bruce has drawn on his lifetime's experience not only traveling in the astral dimension, but teaching others to do so.

Book	Title/Author	Summary
	Astral Projection: A Guide on How to Travel the Astral Plane and Have an Out-Of-Body Experience Mari Silva September 10, 2020	Are you ready to embark on a wholesome Out-of-Body Experience (OBE) to attain a higher level of enlightenment, awareness, and spirituality?
	Adventures Beyond the Body: How to Experience Out-of-Body Travel William Buhlman December 31, 1995	America's leading expert on out-of-body travel tells the riveting story of his travels to other realms and offers easy-to-use techniques to guide you on your journey of a lifetime and beyond.
	My Big TOE - Awakening, Discovery, Inner Workings : The Complete Trilogy Unifying Philosophy, Physics, and Metaphysics Thomas Campbell November 30, 2007	My Big TOE, written by a nuclear physicist in the language of contemporary Western culture, unifies science and philosophy, physics and metaphysics, mind and matter, purpose and meaning, the normal and the paranormal.
	PHILOSOPHER: A Hero's Journey Robert Edward Grant December 16, 2024	Philosopher unveils the connections between creation and consciousness, demonstrating how these universal forces resonate across art, architecture, and the sciences.

Near Death Experiences: Books

Book	Title/Author	Summary
	The Light After Death - My Journey to Heaven and Back Vincent Todd Tolman September 10, 2022	Vincent Tolman was pronounced dead and put in a body bag. Nearly an hour later, he miraculously came back to life. This book is about Vincent's experience.
	Evidence of the Afterlife: The Science of Near-Death Experiences Dr. Jeffrey Long January 18, 2010	"There is currently more scientific evidence to the reality of near death experience (NDE) than there is for how to effectively treat certain forms of cancer," states radiation oncologist Dr. Jeffrey Long
	Touching the Source: A Remarkable Disclosure Eugene Dickerson January 8, 2023	After numerous direct encounters with what humans refer to as a higher power or a god, Eugene Dickerson accepted that his life would never be the same again and vowed to share his experiences with the world.
	Life After Life: The Bestselling Original Investigation That Revealed "Near-Death Experiences" Raymond Moody 1975	Life After Life introduced the world to transformative insights into near-death experiences. This bestselling book has remained a classic work for over 50 years.
	Life and Other Near-Death Experiences Camille Pagán October 31, 2015	From critically acclaimed author Camille Pagán comes a hilarious and hopeful story about a woman choosing between a "perfect" life and actually living.

Videos and Podcasts

Host/Teacher	Links	Summary
Darius J. Wright		"My mission is to empower the realm's consciousness to awaken to their eternal soul and remember who they are and where they came from."
Thomas Campbell		Physicist, consciousness researcher, author of the My Big TOE trilogy and international lecturer, describes the nature of our larger reality, provides a complete theory of consciousness, and explains our purpose and connection to that larger reality.
William Buhlman		The author's forty years of extensive personal out-of-body explorations give him a unique and thought provoking insight into this subject.
Jade Shaw		Jade is an Out of Body Experience (OBE) researcher and Astral Projection teacher that advocates expanded states of consciousness for personal and collective change.

Host/Teacher	Links	Summary
Alex Ferrari		A spiritual series of interviews focused on exploring the deeper mysteries of existence, encouraging self-discovery, and helping people connect with their higher selves.
Eliot and Jesse		Twin brothers who are passionate about sharing stories of Near-Death Experiences
Corey Brandon		Corey created this channel to share his experiences and connect with those who share the same interest and passion for what we in the community call, "Home". Here he documents his OBEs.
Sir Robert Edward Grant		Grant is known for bridging the gap between science, spirituality, and innovation, applying his deep understanding of sacred geometry and universal mathematics to solve problems across diverse industries.

Online Communities & Resources
(Rated by: beginners 1, advanced seekers 2, specialized interest 3)

Community	Rank	Links	Summary
MONROE INSTITUTE	1,2,3		Helping people create more meaningful and joyful lives through the guided exploration of expanded consciousness.
CONSCIOUSNESS HUB	1,2		This is a space for exploring consciousness, personal growth, and the evolution of who we are.
AstralInfo.org	1,2,3		How we can use out-of-body experiences to explore our spiritual identity and enhance our intellectual and physical lives
NDERF Near-Death Experience Research Foundation	1,2		Research and study consciousness experiences and spread the message of love, unity and peace around the world.
Meetup	1		Meet other local people interested in Spiritual Awakening : share experiences, inspire and encourage each other!
COMMUNITY FOR HIGHER CONSCIOUSNESS	2		Their purpose is to support people to be their best selves through moving into higher consciousness.
awakening together	3		An assembly of equals joined in common purpose: Awakening to one true self.

These are only a handful of the many resources now available in bookstores, online, and across countless digital platforms. A quick search on YouTube, X, or even through a simple web search will uncover an endless flow of information and personal stories. You will encounter three categories in your search: scientific, experiential, and spiritual, just choose according to what you resonate with.

The consciousness movement is expanding rapidly, with new voices joining the conversation every day. Perhaps the next story to be told will be yours!

www.ingramcontent.com/pod-product-compliance
Lightning Source LLC
Chambersburg PA
CBHW051549120626
46551CB00013B/1441